THE NEXT GOAT

NIKOLA JOKIĆ

CORINA JEFFRIES

PowerKiDS press

Published in 2025 by The Rosen Publishing Group, Inc.
2544 Clinton Street, Buffalo, NY 14224

First Edition

Editor: Greg Roza
Book Design: Rachel Rising

Photo Credits: Cover, pp. 11,13 ZUMA Press, Inc. / Alamy Stock Photo; Cover, pp. 1,3, 4, 6, 8, 10, 12, 14, 16, 18, 20, 22, 23, 24 Pixacon/Shutterstock.com; Cover Farhanz9/Shutterstock.com; Cover, p. 1 Alhovik/Shutterstock.com; p. 4 JULWITUL TONGBAI/Shutterstock.com; p. 5 Xinhua / Alamy Stock Photo; pp. 7, 15, 21 ASSOCIATED PRESS/AP Images; p. 8 holly_molly/Shutterstock.com; p. 9 Esin Deniz/Shutterstock.com; p. 10 AlexVector/Shutterstock.com; p. 12 Marcelo Mollaretti/Shutterstock.com; p. 17 Marty Jean-Louis / Alamy Stock; p.18 esfera/Shutterstock.com; p. 19 Mariano Garcia / Alamy Stock Photo; p. 20 lev radin/Shutterstock.com.

Library of Congress Cataloging-in-Publication Data

Names: Jeffries, Corina, author.
Title: Nikola Jokić/ Corina Jeffries.
Description: Buffalo : PowerKids Press, [2025] | Series: The next GOAT | Includes index.
Identifiers: LCCN 2024033146 (print) | LCCN 2024033147 (ebook) | ISBN 9781499449761 (lib. bdg.) | ISBN 9781499449754 (pbk.) | ISBN 9781499449778 (ebook)
Subjects: LCSH: Jokić, Nikola, 1995–Juvenile literature. | Centers (Basketball)–Serbia–Biography–Juvenile literature. | Basketball players–Serbia–Biography–Juvenile literature. | Denver Nuggets (Basketball team)–Juvenile literature. | Basketball–Colorado–Denver–History–Juvenile literature. | Olympic athletes–Serbia–Juvenile literature.
Classification: LCC GV884.J65 J44 2025 (print) | LCC GV884.J65 (ebook) | DDC 796.323092 [B]–dc23/eng/20240816
LC record available at https://lccn.loc.gov/2024033146
LC ebook record available at https://lccn.loc.gov/2024033147

Manufactured in the United States of America

Some of the images in this book illustrate individuals who are models. The depictions do not imply actual situations or events.

CPSIA Compliance Information: Batch #CWPK25. For Further Information contact Rosen Publishing at 1-800-237-9932.

CONTENTS

MEET NIKOLA!

Many sports fans believe that Serbian-born basketball player Nikola Jokić is the greatest player ever to play in the National Basketball Association (NBA). In his first 10 seasons, he was named the league's Most **Valuable** Player (MVP) three times. He also led the Denver Nuggets to win the 2023 NBA Championship and has played very well for the Serbian national team.

The story of Jokić's quick rise in the NBA is an exciting one. Read on to learn more about "The Joker."

This photograph shows the Denver Nuggets after winning the 2023 NBA Finals. In one hand, Jokić is holding the trophy, or prize, for the NBA Finals MVP. In the other, he's holding his young daughter, Ognjena.

GROWING UP, GROWING TALL!

Nikola Jokić was born on February 19, 1995, in Sombor, Serbia. He was born with natural **athletic** talent, but he wasn't always interested in sports. Although he was taller than most of his classmates, he was also overweight and didn't enjoy **physical** activities.

His two older brothers, Strahinja and Nemanja, enjoyed basketball. Eventually, Jokić became interested too. He was also into horse racing, but basketball became his main interest. It didn't hurt that he grew to 6 feet 11 inches (211 cm) tall!

WHAT THEY'RE SAYING

"I didn't love physical activities [when I was younger]. In high school, I couldn't do one push-up."

—Nikola Jokić

When he was young, NBA games weren't televised in Serbia. Jokić's interest in basketball grew when he began watching YouTube clips of NBA greats Magic Johnson and Michael Jordan.

KK MEGA BASKET

Although Jokić didn't start playing basketball until his early teens, it was clear that he had great skill. When he was just 17, he moved to Belgrade, the capital of Serbia, to join his first professional league. He played for KK Mega Basket of the Adriatic Basketball Association (ABA). His first year, he played for the junior team and won the league MVP award.

Jokić was a member of the 2013 Serbian national team. He played in the under-19 **tournament**. The team came in second place.

During this time, Jokić also played some games in the Serbian League, Serbia's top basketball league.

Jokić played so well that he earned a spot on the Mega Basket's senior team. He improved greatly during the 2013–2014 season. The 2014–2015 season was even better. Jokić averaged 15.4 points a game. He led the league in rebounds and assists per game. He was named MVP four times during the season and was officially named the ABA MVP in March 2015.

Jokić was famous in Serbia! However, he would soon become a star on a larger stage.

A rebound is when a player grabs the ball after a missed shot. An assist is when a player passes the ball to a teammate, who then scores points.

THE NBA DRAFT

Jokić didn't go to a U.S. college, like many NBA players do. **Scouts** in Europe began to take notice of his excellent skills and the word spread.

In 2014, the Denver Nuggets invited Jokić to play five summer games with the team. Then, on June 26, the Nuggets selected Jokić 41st in the NBA **Draft**. Although they drafted Jokić, they had to wait another year while he finished playing for Mega Basket. Jokić signed a contract with the Nuggets on July 28, 2015.

Although the NBA Draft is televised, Jokić's draft occurred during a Taco Bell commercial! Jokić said that he slept through the draft anyway.

THE DENVER NUGGETS

At first, Jokić didn't stand out in the NBA. He did play well enough, though, to earn a place on the NBA All-Rookie First Team. (Rookie means first year.)

In his fourth season (2018–2019), Jokić scored 20.1 points per game and grabbed 10.8 rebounds per game. For the 2021–2022 season, Jokić scored 27.1 points per game! That year, he won his second NBA MVP award. Despite the success, Jokić and the Nuggets still struggled to reach the NBA Championship Game.

WHAT THEY'RE SAYING

"[Jokić] has an unbelievable talent of seeing the floor and seeing plays happen before they happen."

—NBA superstar LeBron James

Even though the Nuggets faltered in the playoffs each year, Jokić earned a spot on the All-Star team four times in four years (2019–2022).

2023 NBA CHAMPS

The 2022–2023 season was the greatest of Jokić's career to date. The Nuggets ended the regular season with a record of 53 wins and 29 losses. Jokić nearly became the first player to average a triple-double for a single season. He averaged 24.5 points a game, 11.8 rebounds a game, and 9.8 assists a game!

During the playoffs, Jokić had 10 triple-doubles, which broke NBA great Wilt Chamberlain's record of seven. The Nuggets beat the Miami Heat to win the NBA Finals. Jokić earned the NBA Finals' MVP award.

WHAT THEY'RE SAYING

"[Jokić is] the Most Valuable Player every time he steps on the court."
—Jamal Murray, Nuggets guard and Jokić's teammate

A triple-double is when a player reaches "double digits" (10 and over) in three of five categories in a single game—points, assists, rebounds, steals, and blocked shots.

THE SERBIAN NATIONAL TEAM

Jokić has played for the Serbian national team in numerous international **competitions**. He found early success with the under-19 Serbian national team in 2013. Jokić led the team to second place, losing to the United States.

In 2016, the Serbian national team **qualified** for the Summer Olympics for the first time. Jokić won the MVP award for the 2016 **FIBA** World Olympic Qualifying Tournament. Serbia again came in second, losing to the United States in the final round.

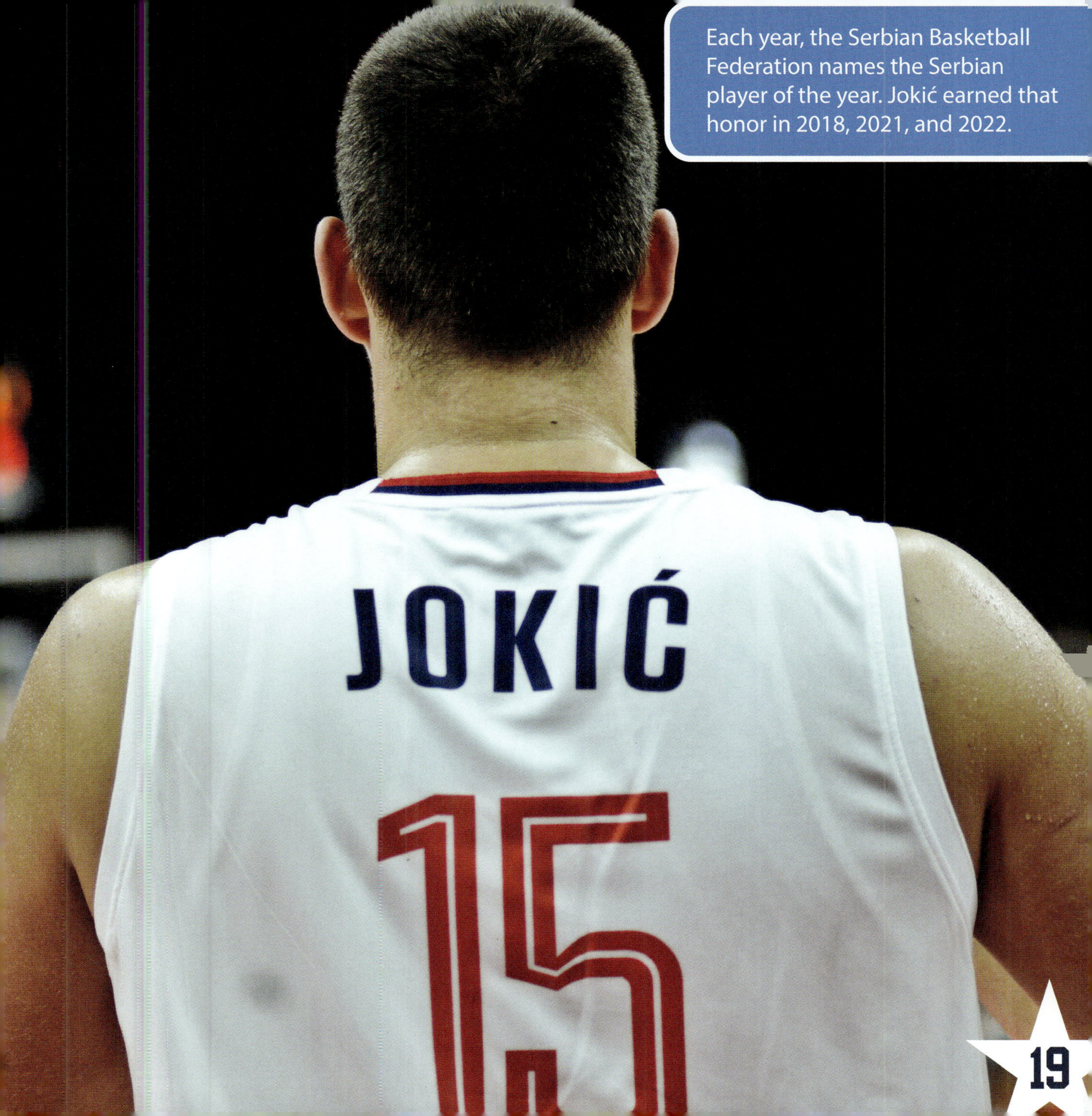

Each year, the Serbian Basketball Federation names the Serbian player of the year. Jokić earned that honor in 2018, 2021, and 2022.

WHAT'S NEXT?

Nikola Jokić continues to amaze fans. The Nuggets nearly made it to the NBA Finals again in 2024, and he once again won the NBA MVP award.

He and his wife, Natalija Jokić, had a little girl in September 2021. Ognjena (which means "fire" in Serbian) was just 2 years old when Nikola and Nuggets won the 2023 NBA Finals. In fact, she was there to celebrate with her dad!

Nikola Jokić is sure to continue to amaze fans and family members alike.

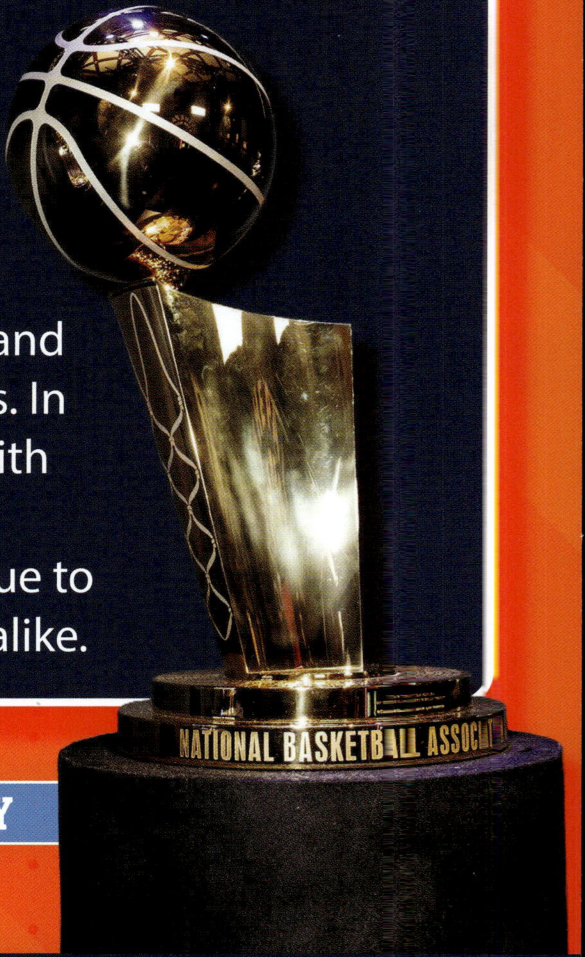

LARRY O'BRIEN CHAMPIONSHIP TROPHY

People are already saying that Nikola Jokić will be the greatest Denver Nuggets player of all time. Others think he will become the greatest NBA player of all time!

GLOSSARY

athletic: Physically strong, fit, and active.

competition: An event at which athletes compete.

draft: A process of selecting young players to be members of the teams in a league.

FIBA: International Basketball Federation, the ruling body that governs basketball worldwide.

physical: Having to do with the body and its movement.

qualify: In sports, to play well enough to make it to the next level.

scout: Someone who observes young athletes in the hope of finding new players for a team.

tournament: A contest or series of contests played for a championship.

valuable: Important.

FOR MORE INFORMATION

BOOKS

Coleman, Ted. *Denver Nuggets All-Time Greats*. Mendota Heights, MN: Press Box Books, 2023.

Stabler, David. *Meet Nikola Jokić: Denver Nuggets Superstar.* Minneapolis, MN: Learner Publications, 2024.

Whiting, Jim. *The Story of the Denver Nuggets*. Mankato, MN: Creative Paperbacks, 2023.

WEBSITES

Kiddle: Nikola Jokić Facts for Kids
kids.kiddle.co/Nikola_Jokić
Read much more about this incredible basketball player.

Denver Nuggets Official Website
www.nba.com/nuggets
Keep up with the Denver Nuggets at their official website.

Publisher's note to educators and parents: Our editors have carefully reviewed these websites to ensure that they are suitable for students. Many websites change frequently, however, and we cannot guarantee that a site's future contents will continue to meet our high standards of quality and educational value. Be advised that students should be closely supervised whenever they access the internet.

INDEX